Overview

In simple ter
where the same design is repeated at different sizes. We will be making a quilt with the design shown below:

Figure 1 The quilt design

You should be able to see that it consists of a repeating friendship star pattern, in three different sizes. In these instructions, we will be colour coding the pattern to easily distinguish between the different sizes. Against the cream background, we have a large star in purple, some medium stars in green, and many small stars in brown. Of course, the actual colours you choose are entirely up to you, and there isn't even a need to pick three different colours. This quilt would work just as well in monochrome.

Because the friendship star is repeated in three different sizes, it's important to pay careful attention to the cutting instructions. Some of the steps will look suspiciously similar to earlier steps, but the measurements will be different.

The small stars

1. Cut a piece approximately 1m from both the small star fabric and the background fabric.

2. On the wrong side of the fabric for the small stars, mark a diagonal line 3" from a corner. Make sure the line is at 45° to the selvedge. There will probably be a 45° line on one of your rulers to help with this. This marking can be done with an ordinary pencil as it will be on the edge of a seam allowance.

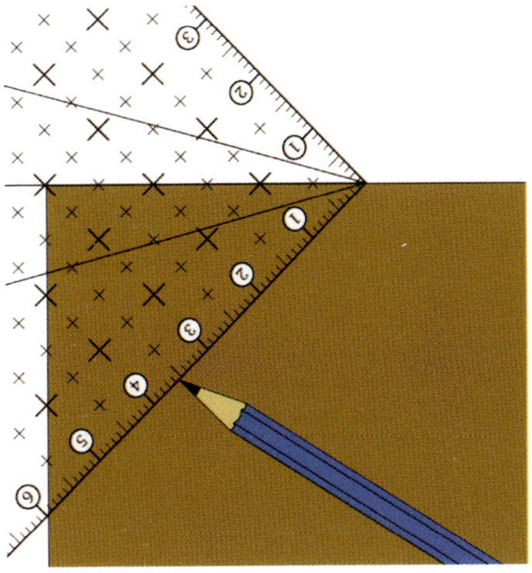

Figure 2 Marking the diagonal line

3. Mark several more lines parallel to this, each 3" from the last line. You will almost certainly need the whole of this piece to make enough half square triangles but I hate wasting fabric so I prefer to mark and sew in sections.

Figure 3 Marking the parallel lines

4. Place the star fabric right sides together with the background fabric and pin together in a few places. Keep the pins well away from the lines.

5. With a slightly shorter than normal stitch length sew slightly less than ¼" from each side of each line.

6. Press the sewn fabrics to get them flat again.

7. Cut along every line that has stitching on each side of it.

8. On a small ruler use a piece of masking tape to join the 3½" marks on two adjacent sides of the ruler.

Figure 4 Stitching either side of the line

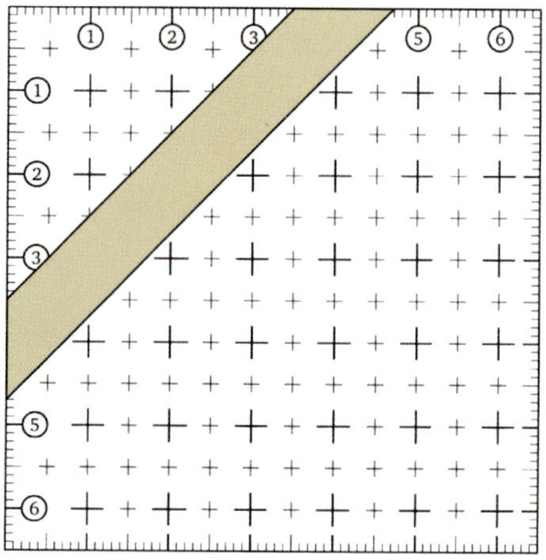

Figure 5 Marking the ruler with masking tape

9. Align the masking tape with the stitching lines on one of the sewn fabric tubes, and cut along both edges of the ruler. On the longer strips you can cut triangles from both sides of the strip to get the most out of each piece.

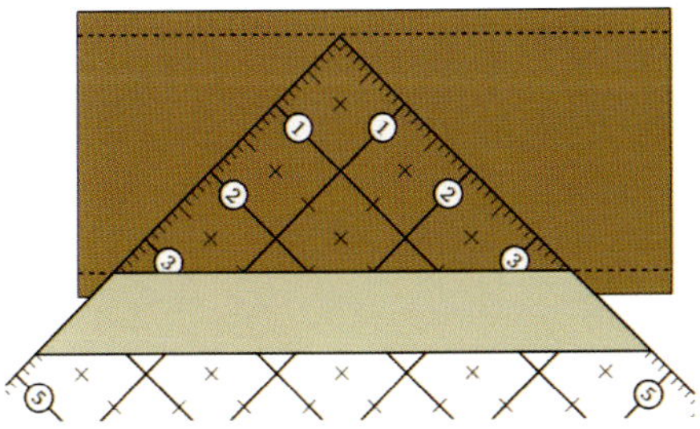

Figure 6 Aligning the ruler to cut the triangles

10. Repeat this process until you have made one hundred of these triangle units.

11. Open the triangles and press so the seams are behind the darker fabric.

12. Cut nine strips the full width of the fabric and 3½" wide.

13. Sub cut these strips into one hundred and twenty five 3½" x 3½" squares.

14. Lay out stacks of pieces in the pattern of the block, as shown in figure 7. Make sure all the half square triangles in each stack are in the same orientation.

15. Join the top three pieces together into a row. Repeat for the middle and bottow rows.

16. Press these three rows so that the seams on the top and bottom rows go behind the outside pieces and the middle row so the seams are under the center piece. This will allow them to nestle together when we join the rows. See figure 8

Figure 7 Laying out the small star

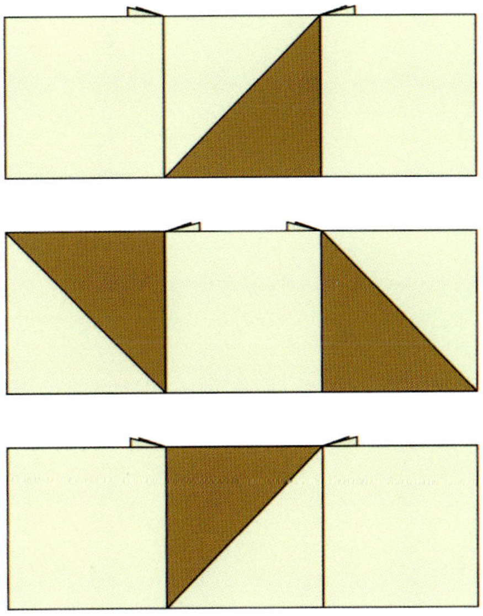

Figure 8 Pressing the small star

17. Join the rows together to make the small star block. You may want to pin at the junctions to ensure accuracy.

18. Repeat steps 15 to 17 with the remaining pieces.

Figure 9 The full quilt, with an extra border

The medium stars

19. Cut 1m of background fabric and 1m of fabric for the medium stars.

20. On the wrong side of the fabric for the medium stars mark a diagonal line 7¼" from a corner. Make sure the line is at 45° to the selvedge, there will probably be a 45° line on one of your rulers. This marking can be done with an ordinary pencil as it will be on the edge of a seam allowance.

21. Mark several more lines parallel to this each 7¼" from the last line. As before, you will almost certainly need the whole of this piece to make enough half

Figure 10 Marking the diagonal line

square triangles, but I prefer to mark and sew in sections.

Figure 11 Marking parallel lines

22. Place the star fabric right sides together with the background fabric and pin together in a few places. Keep the pins well away from the lines.

23. With a slightly shorter than normal stitch length sew slightly less than ¼" from each side of each line.

24. Press the sewn fabrics to get them flat again.

25. Cut along each line that has stitching on each side of it.

26. The easiest way to do the next steps are with a large square ruler, the same way that you did for the smaller stars. If you have a large enough square ruler, use a piece of masking tape to join the 9½" marks on two adjacent sides of the ruler.

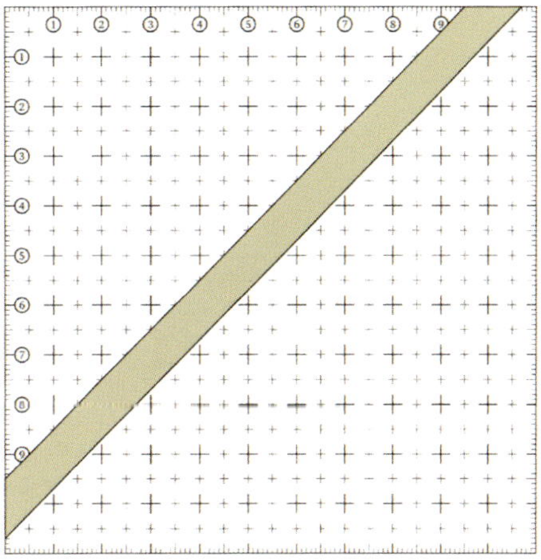

Figure 12
Marking the ruler

27. Align the masking tape with the stitching lines on one of the sewn fabric tubes, and cut along both edges of the ruler. On the longer strips you can cut triangles from both sides of the strip to get the most out of each piece. Skip to step 31.

28. If you don't have a large square ruler, then you can use any ruler

that is at least 10" long and 5" wide, using a slightly different technique. Most rulers will have a 45° angle marked on them. If it does, you can use that. If not, you'll need to mark a 45° line from one of the corners using masking tape.

29. Align the 45° line on the ruler with the seam line as shown, and draw along the long edge of the ruler. Mark the point 9½" along the ruler.

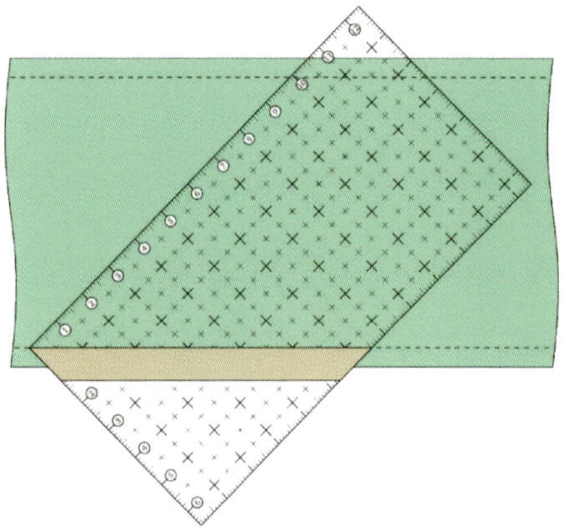

Figure 13 Using a narrow ruler

30. Align the ruler to make the third edge of the triangle. The short edge should be parallel to the previously drawn line. If your seams are straight, the new line you're marking will be 9½" long. If it's not, you might need to fiddle with the ruler positioning slightly until it is 9½". Mark the third edge of the triangle and cut along the marked lines.

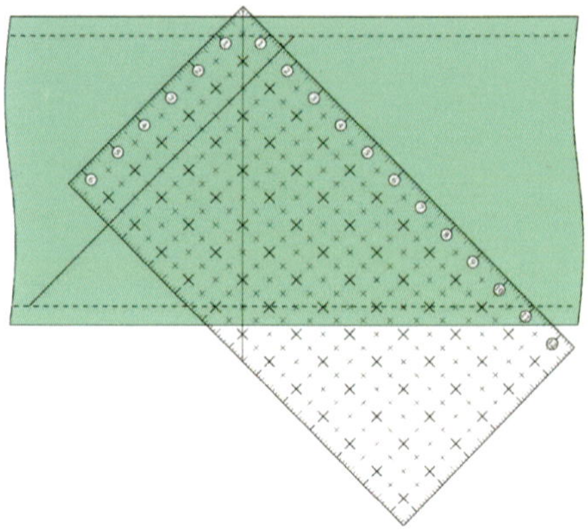

Figure 14 Using a narrow ruler

31. Repeat this process until you have made twenty of these triangle units. Press the units open so that the seams are behind the darker fabric.

32. Lay out the medium stars interspersed with the small star blocks you made earler, as shown:

Figure 15 Laying out the medium star

33. Join these pieces to make five blocks using the same method we used for the small stars.

Figure 16 The full quilt, using Ricky Tims hand dyes

The large star

34. Cut three strips of the background fabric, the full width of the fabric and 9½" wide.

35. Sub cut these strips into twelve 9½" x 9½" squares.

36. Similarly, cut three strips of the large star fabric, the full width of the fabric and 9½" wide.

37. Sub cut these strips into twelve 9½" x 9½" squares.

38. Cut ¾m of background fabric and ¾m of fabric for the large stars. Repeat steps 20 to 31 using the large star fabric instead of the medium star fabric, and this time only make twelve half

square triangle units instead of the twenty you made before.

39. Assemble the four large star points as shown, using the same method as for the small stars.

Figure 17 Assembling the large star points

40. Join the four large star point blocks with the five previously assembled small/medium star blocks to complete the quilt top.

Figure 18 Laying out the large blocks

Border

The top is now complete and you can press and quilt it as is. However, if you would like a larger quilt or if you would prefer to frame the central design, you can add extra borders as necessary. You can add any design you choose, whether it be just a simple extra border of the background fabric or something more intricate. The instructions given here are for the border shown in figure 9.

41. We'll need to make some more half square triangles the same size that were used to make the small stars. Cut a piece of the small star fabric 10" x 24".

42. As in steps 2 and 3, mark diagonal lines on the wrong side of the fabric, 3" apart.

43. Place it right sides together with a similar 10" x 24" piece of the background fabric and sew the two together, ¼" from each side of the marked lines.

44. Press the fabrics flat.

45. Cut along each marked line that has stitching either side of it.

46. Mark the 3½" diagonal on a small ruler, as shown in figure 5.

47. Use this ruler to cut twenty triangles from your strips, aligning the masking take with the seams, just as you did in step 9 while making the small stars.

48. Cut a 14" x 14" square of the medium star fabric.

49. As before, mark diagonal lines on the wrong side of the fabric, 3" apart.

50. Cut a 14" x 14" square of the background fabric and place it right sides together with the medium star fabric.

51. Sew the two together, ¼" from the marked lines.

52. Cut along the marked lines.

53. Cut sixteen triangles using the ruler as in step 47.

54. Open and press the sixteen medium star fabric triangles and the twenty small star fabric triangles, pressing towards the darker fabric.

55. Cut six strips of background fabric, 3½" by the full width of the fabric.

56. Cut five of the strips into six 6½" lengths.

57. From the remaining strip, cut two 6½" lengths and eight 3½" squares.

58. Take one of the small star fabric triangles and attach it to one of the 3½" squares of background fabric that you've just cut as shown. Note that the orientation is important here. Make sure you attach the square to the triangle exactly as shown.

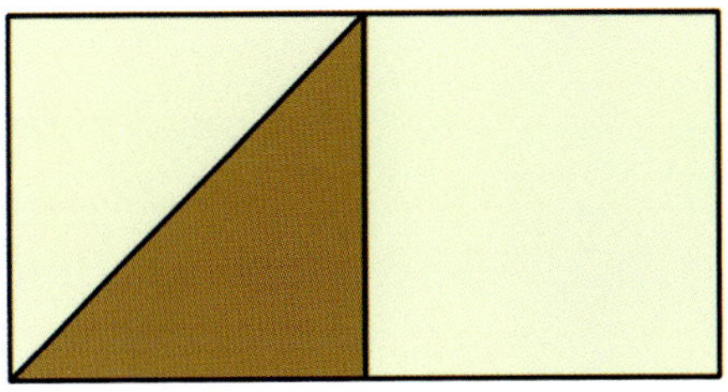

Figure 19 Attaching a square to a triangle

59. Repeat this another three times, so that you have four square/triangle pieces.

60. For each of the remaining triangles, both those made with the small star fabric and those made with the medium star fabric, attach a 6½" x 3½" rectangle of background fabric as shown in figure 20. Again, the orientation is important.

61. From the pieces you've just made, take one made with the small star fabric and one made with the medium star fabric, and join them together as shown.

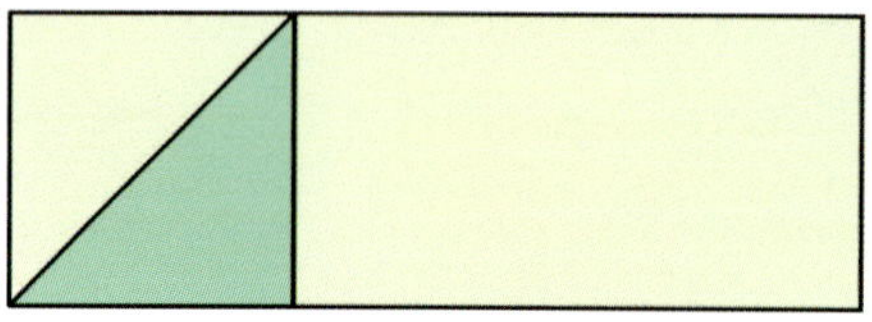

Figure 20 Attaching a rectangle to a triangle

You'll need to do this sixteen times.

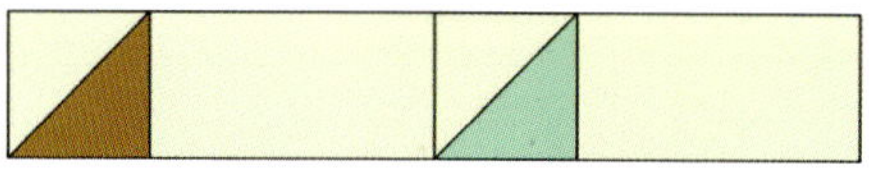

Figure 21 Joining the border pieces

62. Join four of these pieces together.

63. Attach the triangle/square piece you made in step 58 to the background rectangle at the right hand end of the strip.

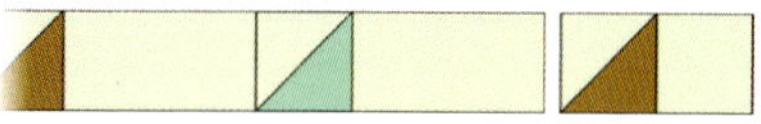

Figure 22 The right hand end of the border strip

64. Attach one of the 3½" background squares you made in step 57 to the small star triangle at the left hand end of the strip.

Figure 23 The left hand end of the border strip

65. Repeat steps 62 to 64 another three times, so you now have four border strips.

66. Cut eight strips of the large star fabric, 2" by 41". You should be able to get 41" of usable fabric across the full width of a bolt. However, on some narrow fabrics, you might not quite be able to get the full 41". If that's the case, then cut 39" strips.

67. If you had to cut 39" strips due to narrow fabric, cut a ninth strip, and from that, cut four 2" x 4½" lengths.

68. Join two 41" strips to make an 81½" strip. If you had to cut 39" strips, then join two of them together with a 4½" length between the two.

69. Repeat this another three times, so you end up with four 81½" long strips.

70. Cut eight strips of the large star fabric, 3" by 41". Again, if you're unable to get 41" from your width of fabric, cut 39" strips instead and cut a ninth strip and cut hour 4½" lengths from it to make up the difference.

71. Join two 41" strips to make an 81½" strip. If you had to cut 39" strips, then join two of

them together with a 4½" length between the two.

72. Repeat this three times, so you have another four 81½" long strips.

73. Take one strip of triangles and rectangles, and one each of the narrow and wider strips of the large star fabric, and join them as shown below, with the narrow strip below the triangles and the wider strip on top.

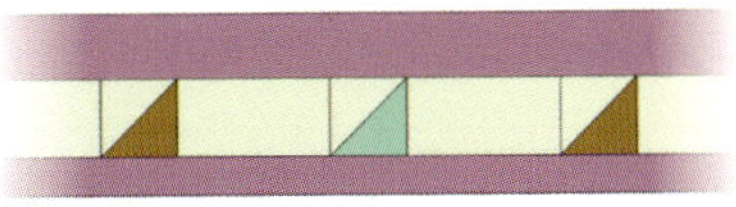

Figure 24 Joining the border strips together

74. From the large star fabric, cut four 7½" squares.

75. Take two of your border strips and add a square to each end, so that you have two long border strips with squares and two shorter strips without squares.

76. Join the shorter strips to the left and right sides of the quilt top.

77. Join the longer strips to the top and bottom of the quilt top.

78. The quilt is now complete and ready to be pressed and quilted.

About fractals

The discovery of fractals can be traced back as far as the 17th century, and much progress was made in understanding their mathematical properties in the late 19th century.

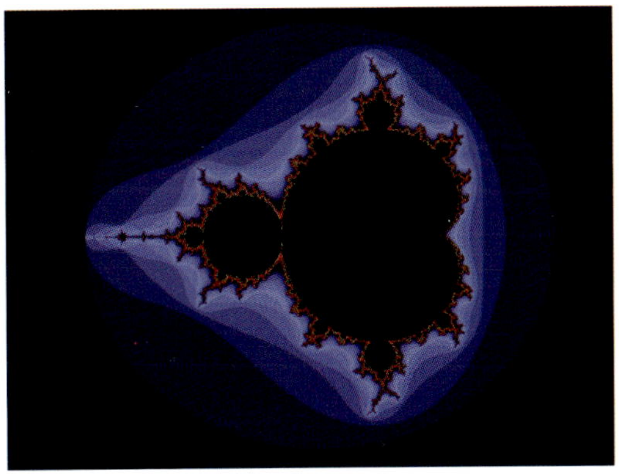

Figure 25 The Mandelbrot set

However, fractals in the sense that most understand them today, are primarily down to the work of French-American mathematician Benoît B. Mandelbrot, and it was Mandelbrot that coined the term fractal, to describe in his own words "a rough or fragmented geometric shape that can be split into parts, each of which is (at least approximately) a reduced-size copy of the whole".

Although their mathematical properties had been understood for a long time, it was access to powerful computers while working for IBM that allowed Mandelbrot to produce visualizations of the fractals on which

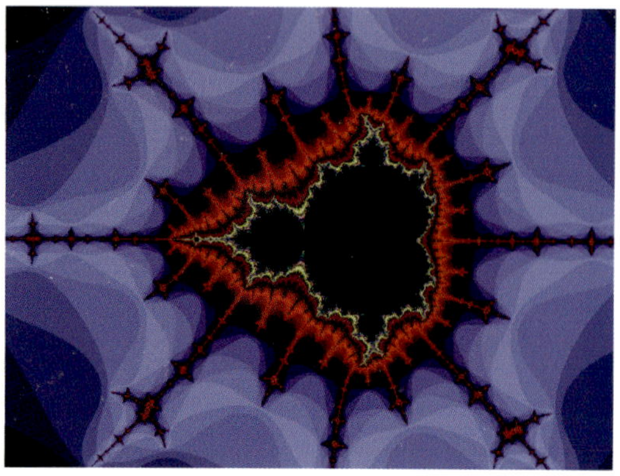

Figure 26 A close up of part of the Mandelbrot set

Figure 28 A Barnsley fern fractal

he'd been working, and thus bring them to a much wider audience. The most famous fractal is the Mandelbrot set, a part of which has been used in the margins of this pattern.

Zooming in to a section of the Mandelbrot set reveals another shape with the same amount of detail, similar to the shape of the set as a whole, as shown in figure 26.

Each point on the Mandelbrot set has an equivalent Julia set, named after the mathematician Gaston Julia.

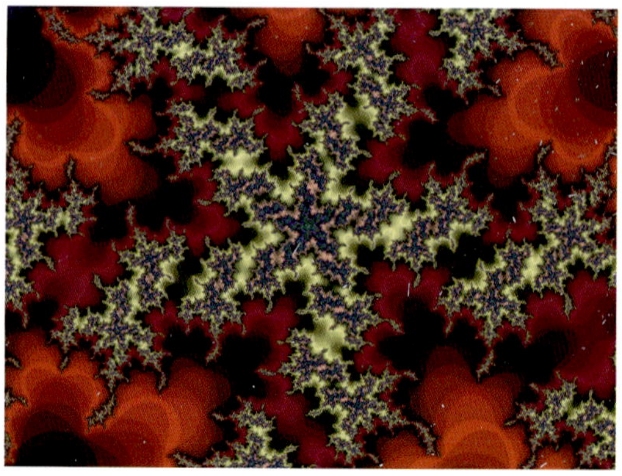

Figure 27 A Julia set corresponding to a point on the Mandelbrot set

Figure 29 A Newton-Raphson fractal

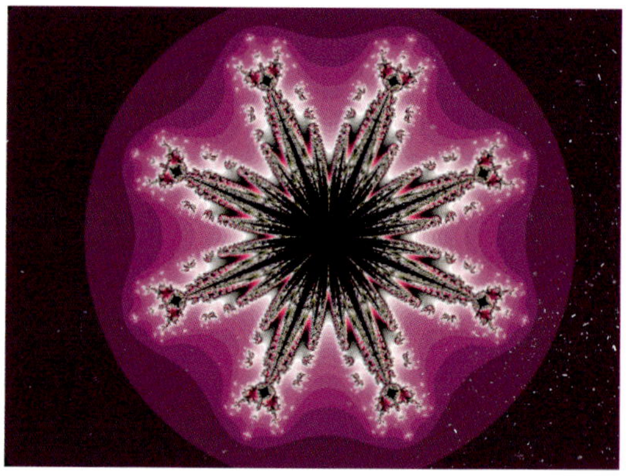

Figure 30 An octal fractal

Although the Mandelbrot set is the most well known fractal, a variety of others are illustrated on this page.